Delicious
pizza

Delicious

pizza

Love Food ™ is an imprint of Parragon Books Ltd

Parragon
Queen Street House
4 Queen Street
Bath BA1 1HE, UK

Copyright © Parragon Books Ltd 2008

Photography by Günter Beer
Home economy by Stevan Paul
Introduction and new recipes by Linda Doeser

ISBN 978-1-4054-9560-8

Printed in China

Notes for the reader
• This book uses imperial, metric, and US cup measurements. Follow the same units of measurement throughout; do not mix imperial and metric.
• All spoon measurements are level: teaspoons are assumed to be 5 ml, and tablespoons are assumed to be 15 ml.
• Unless otherwise stated, milk is assumed to be lowfat and eggs are medium. The times given are an approximate guide only.
• Some recipes contain nuts. If you are allergic to nuts you should avoid using them and any products containing nuts.
• Recipes using raw or very lightly cooked eggs should be avoided by infants, the elderly, pregnant women, convalescents, and anyone suffering from illness.

Contents

6   Introduction

8   Classic Toppings

30 Meat Lovers

52 Strictly Vegetarian

74 Something Special

96 Index

Introduction

The word pizza comes from the Italian word "pizzicare," meaning to be hot or spicy, and it is thought that the original pizza consisted of a bread dough base drizzled liberally with olive oil and sprinkled with garlic, oregano, and fiery hot peperoncino chiles. It was only in the nineteenth century when the city of Naples created a pizza to honor Queen Margherita that tomatoes and cheese—those staples of pizza toppings—were introduced. As Italians, particularly Neapolitans, moved across Europe and North America they opened pizzerias in all the major cities and this humble snack food became a global phenomenon.

Pizza toppings have become increasingly varied and interesting as cooks around the world have experimented with local ingredients. Modern toppings also tend to include more ingredients than the pizzas of the past. If Italy had a queen to honor now,

tomatoes, cheese, and basil would probably seem a somewhat inadequate way to commemorate a royal visit. Nevertheless, the classic recipes are still firm favorites with many, as they are quick and easy to prepare and the traditional flavor combinations have stood the test of time.

Making pizza

This book provides a recipe for basic Pizza Dough (see page 11) which takes little time, but it does need to stand for about 1 hour to rise. If you are in a hurry, you can use a ready-made, part-cooked pizza base. These are available from supermarkets and while not quite so delicious as the homemade variety, are still satisfactory.

Many pizza recipes start by covering the pizza base with some kind of tomato sauce. One of the easiest

and most convenient options is to buy a good brand of ready-made pizza sauce. However, making your own is almost as easy. For a basic Tomato Sauce, soften a chopped onion and a finely chopped garlic clove in a tablespoon of olive oil in a pan for 5 minutes. Stir in 7 oz/200 g canned chopped tomatoes, 1–2 teaspoons tomato paste, a pinch of sugar, and a pinch of dried oregano, season with salt and pepper, and simmer gently, stirring occasionally, for 20–25 minutes, until thick and pulpy. Let cool completely before using.

Homemade tomato sauce can be stored in a screw-top jar in the refrigerator for up to a week. You could also use strained canned tomatoes and even tomato paste, although this has a very intense flavor and is probably better diluted with a little water first. Peeled and finely diced fresh tomatoes may also be used, creating a different texture. Of course, not all pizzas include tomatoes or tomato sauce.

The recipes in this book suggest a huge variety of different toppings to suit all tastes. They are all easy to follow and have been divided into four chapters, making it easy to find exactly the one you want. Classic Toppings speaks for itself and includes traditional meat, vegetarian, and shellfish pizzas. The toppings in Meat Lovers range from creamy chicken to spicy pepperoni and meatballs—the perfect choice when you're really hungry. Strictly Vegetarian suggests some delicious new ways with vegetables as well as some favorite combinations, while the recipes in Something Special are ideal for those days when you want something a little different.

Classic
Toppings

serves 2–4

¹/2 oz/15 g fresh yeast or
1 tsp dried or active dry yeast

6 tbsp lukewarm water

¹/2 tsp sugar

1 tbsp olive oil, plus extra
for oiling

1¹/2 cups all-purpose flour,
plus extra for dusting

1 tsp salt

pizza dough

Combine the fresh yeast with the water and sugar in a bowl. If using dried yeast, sprinkle it over the surface of the water and whisk in until dissolved.

Set aside in a warm place for 10–15 minutes until frothy on the surface. Stir in the olive oil.

Sift the flour and salt into a large bowl. If using easy-blend yeast, stir it in. Make a well in the center and pour in the yeast liquid, or water and oil (without the sugar for active dry yeast).

Using either floured hands or a wooden spoon, mix together to form a dough. Turn out onto a floured counter and knead for about 5 minutes or until smooth and elastic.

Place the dough in a large oiled plastic bag and set aside in a warm place for about 1 hour or until doubled in size. Airing cupboards are often the best places for this process, as the temperature remains constant.

Turn out onto a lightly floured counter and punch down the dough. This releases any air bubbles which would make the pizza uneven. Knead 4 or 5 times. The dough is now ready to use.

serves 2–4

2 tbsp olive oil, plus extra for brushing

1 quantity Pizza Dough (see page 11), or 1 x 10-inch/25-cm pizza base

all-purpose flour, for dusting

6 tomatoes, thinly sliced

6 oz/175 g mozzarella cheese, drained and thinly sliced

2 tbsp shredded fresh basil leaves

salt and pepper

margarita pizza

Preheat the oven to 450°F/230°C. Brush a cookie sheet with oil.

Roll out the dough on a lightly floured counter to a 10-inch round. Place on the cookie sheet and push up the edge a little. Cover and let stand in a warm place for 10 minutes.

Arrange the tomato and mozzarella slices alternately over the pizza base. Season to taste with salt and pepper, sprinkle with the basil, and drizzle with the olive oil.

Bake in the oven for 15–20 minutes, until the crust is crisp and the cheese has melted.

serves 2–4

2 tbsp olive oil, plus extra for brushing

1 quantity Pizza Dough (see page 11), or 1 x 10-inch/ 25-cm pizza base

all-purpose flour, for dusting

14 oz/400 g canned chopped tomatoes

5 oz/150 g cured ham, diced

7 oz/200 g canned pineapple slices in juice, drained

1/2 cup grated Monterey jack cheese

hawaiian pizza

Preheat the oven to 400°F/200°C. Brush a cookie sheet with oil.

Roll out the dough on a lightly floured counter to a 10-inch/ 25-cm round. Place on the cookie sheet and push up the edge a little. Cover and let stand in a warm place for 10 minutes.

Spoon the tomatoes over the base almost to the edge, then sprinkle evenly with the ham.

Cut the pineapple slices into bite-size pieces and sprinkle them over the pizza. Sprinkle with the grated cheese and bake for 20 minutes, until the edge is crisp and golden. Serve immediately.

serves 2–4

olive oil, for brushing

1 quantity Pizza Dough (see page 11), or 1 x 10-inch pizza base

all-purpose flour, for dusting

2 tbsp butter or margarine

4³/₄ cups sliced mixed mushrooms

2 garlic cloves, crushed

2 tbsp chopped fresh parsley, plus extra to garnish

2 tbsp tomato paste

6 tbsp sieved tomatoes

³/₄ cup grated mozzarella cheese

salt and pepper

garlic mushroom pizza

Preheat the oven to 375°F/190°C. Brush a cookie sheet with oil.

Roll out the dough on a lightly floured counter to a 10-inch/25-cm round. Place on the cookie sheet and push up the edge a little. Cover and let stand in a warm place for 10 minutes.

Melt the butter or margarine in a skillet and cook the mushrooms, garlic, and parsley over low heat for 5 minutes.

Combine the tomato paste and sieved tomatoes and spoon onto the pizza base, leaving a ½-inch/1-cm edge of dough. Spoon the mushroom mixture on top. Season to taste with salt and pepper and sprinkle the cheese on top.

Cook the pizza in the oven for 20–25 minutes or until the base is crisp and the cheese has melted. Garnish with chopped parsley and serve the pizza immediately.

serves 4

2 loaves of ciabatta or
2 baguettes

1 quantity basic Tomato
Sauce (see page 7)

4 plum tomatoes, thinly
sliced lengthwise

5 1/2 oz/150 g mozzarella
cheese, thinly sliced

10 black olives, cut into rings

8 fresh basil leaves, shredded

olive oil, for drizzling

salt and pepper

tomato & olive pizzas

Cut the bread in half lengthwise and toast the cut side of the bread lightly. Carefully spread the toasted bread with the Tomato Sauce.

Arrange the tomato and mozzarella slices alternately along the length.

Top with the olive rings and half of the basil. Drizzle over a little olive oil and season with salt and pepper.

Either place under a preheated medium broiler and cook until the cheese is melted and bubbling, or bake in a preheated oven, 400°F/200°C, for 15–20 minutes.

Sprinkle over the remaining basil and serve immediately.

serves 2–4

4 tbsp olive oil, plus extra for brushing

2 cups chopped mushrooms

1 garlic clove, thinly sliced (optional)

1 tbsp lemon juice

1 quantity Pizza Dough (see page 11), or 1 x 10-inch/ 25-cm pizza base

all-purpose flour, for dusting

scant 1 cup diced bacon

pinch of dried oregano

1/2 cup grated Cheddar cheese

salt and pepper

tasty bacon pizza

Heat half the olive oil in a pan. Add the mushrooms, garlic, and lemon juice, season with salt and pepper, cover, and cook over low heat, stirring occasionally, for 6 minutes. Remove the pan from the heat and let cool.

Preheat the oven to 400°F/200°C. Brush a cookie sheet with oil.

Roll out the dough on a lightly floured counter to a 10-inch/ 25-cm round. Place on the cookie sheet and push up the edge a little. Cover and let stand in a warm place for 10 minutes.

Brush the pizza base with half the remaining olive oil and spread out the mushrooms evenly on top almost to the edge. Sprinkle with the diced bacon and season with a pinch of dried oregano. Sprinkle the cheese over the pizza, drizzle with the remaining oil, and bake for 20–25 minutes, until crisp and golden. Serve immediately.

serves 2–4

2 tbsp olive oil, plus extra for brushing

1 quantity Pizza Dough (see page 11), or 1 x 10-inch/ 25-cm pizza base

all-purpose flour, for dusting

3/4 cup strained canned tomatoes or 1 quantity basic Tomato Sauce (see page 7)

1 red onion, halved and thinly sliced

2/3 cup freshly grated Parmesan cheese

2 oz/55 g Gorgonzola cheese

2 oz/55 g fontina cheese, thinly sliced

2 oz/55 g goat cheese

1 tbsp pine nuts or capers

salt and pepper

fresh basil sprigs, to garnish

quattro formaggio pizza

Preheat the oven to 400°F/200°C. Brush a cookie sheet with oil.

Roll out the dough on a lightly floured counter to a 10-inch/ 25-cm round. Place on the cookie sheet and push up the edge a little. Cover and let stand in a warm place for 10 minutes.

Brush the pizza base with half the olive oil, then spread the strained canned tomatoes or Tomato Sauce over it almost to the edge. Spread out the onion slices evenly over the top and season with salt and pepper.

Cover one-fourth of the pizza base with grated Parmesan. Crumble the Gorgonzola over a second fourth and arrange the slices of fontina over a third. Depending on the type of goat cheese, either crumble it directly over the remaining fourth or slice it first before adding to the pizza.

Sprinkle the pine nuts or capers over the top and drizzle with the remaining olive oil. Bake for 20–25 minutes, until crisp and golden. Garnish with basil sprigs and serve immediately.

serves 2–4

6–8 canned anchovy fillets, drained and halved lengthwise

2 tbsp milk (optional)

4 tbsp olive oil, plus extra for brushing

1 onion, halved and thinly sliced

2 garlic cloves, finely chopped

14 oz/400 g canned chopped tomatoes

1 tbsp sun-dried tomato paste

pinch of dried oregano

1 tbsp chopped fresh flat-leaf parsley

1 quantity Pizza Dough (see page 11), or 1 x 10-inch/25-cm pizza base

all-purpose flour, for dusting

6 oz/175 g mozzarella cheese, thinly sliced

4–6 pimiento stuffed olives, sliced

salt and pepper

anchovy pizza

If you find anchovies too salty, put them in a shallow saucer, add the milk, and let soak for 10 minutes. Drain and pat dry with paper towels.

Meanwhile, heat 2 tbsp of the olive oil in a pan. Add the onion and cook over low heat, stirring occasionally, for 5 minutes, until softened. Stir in the garlic and cook for 2 minutes more, then add the tomatoes, sun-dried tomato paste, and oregano and season with salt and pepper. Simmer gently, stirring occasionally, for 15–20 minutes, until thickened. Remove the pan from the heat, stir in the parsley, and let cool.

Preheat the oven to 400°F/200°C. Brush a cookie sheet with oil.

Roll out the dough on a lightly floured counter to a 10-inch/25-cm round. Place on the cookie sheet and push up the edge a little. Cover and let stand in a warm place for 10 minutes.

Brush the pizza base with half the remaining oil, then cover evenly with the cooled tomato sauce, spreading it out almost to the edge. Place the slices of mozzarella on top. Make a lattice pattern with the halved anchovy fillets and place a slice of olive on the spaces between. Drizzle with the remaining oil and bake for 20–25 minutes, until crisp and golden. Serve immediately.

serves 2–4

3 tbsp olive oil, plus extra for brushing and drizzling

1 quantity Pizza Dough (see page 11), or 1 x 10-inch/25-cm pizza base

all-purpose flour, for dusting

2 tbsp freshly grated Parmesan cheese

1 quantity basic Tomato Sauce (see page 7)

6 oz/175 g spinach

1 small red onion, thinly sliced

1/4 tsp freshly grated nutmeg

2 hard-cooked eggs

1/4 cup fresh white bread crumbs

1/2 cup grated Jarlsberg, Cheddar, or Swiss cheese, grated

2 tbsp sliced almonds

salt and pepper

florentine pizza

Preheat the oven to 400°F/200°C. Brush a cookie sheet with oil.

Roll out the dough on a lightly floured counter to a 10-inch/25-cm round. Place on the cookie sheet and push up the edge a little. Cover and let stand in a warm place for 10 minutes. Spread the Tomato Sauce almost to the edge.

Remove the stalks from the spinach and wash the leaves thoroughly in plenty of cold water. Drain well and pat off the excess water with paper towels.

Heat the remaining oil and cook the onion for 5 minutes until softened. Add the spinach and cook until just wilted. Drain off any excess liquid. Arrange on the pizza and sprinkle over the nutmeg.

Shell and slice the eggs. Arrange the slices of egg on top of the spinach.

Combine the bread crumbs, cheese, and almonds and sprinkle over. Drizzle with a little olive oil and season to taste.

Bake for 18–20 minutes or until the edge is crisp and golden. Serve the pizza immediately.

serves 2–4

2 tbsp olive oil, plus extra for brushing

1 quantity Pizza Dough (see page 11), or 1 x 10-inch/ 25-cm pizza base

all-purpose flour, for dusting

14 oz/400 g canned chopped tomatoes

7 oz/200 g canned tuna in olive oil, drained

1¼ cups cooked peeled shrimp

scant 1 cup grated mozzarella cheese

1 tbsp chopped fresh parsley

1 tbsp chopped fresh oregano

1 garlic clove, very finely chopped

seafood pizza

Preheat the oven to 400°F/200°C. Brush a cookie sheet with oil.

Roll out the dough on a lightly floured counter to a 10-inch/ 25-cm round. Place on the cookie sheet and push up the edge a little. Cover and let stand in a warm place for 10 minutes.

Spoon the tomatoes evenly over the base almost to the edge. Flake the tuna and spread it over the tomatoes, then arrange the shrimp on top. Sprinkle with the mozzarella.

Combine the parsley, oregano, garlic, and olive oil and drizzle the mixture over the pizza. Bake for 20 minutes, until the edge is crisp and golden. Serve immediately.

2

Meat Lovers

serves 2–4

olive oil, for brushing and drizzling

1 quantity Pizza Dough (see page 11), or 1 x 10-inch/ 25-cm pizza base

all-purpose flour, for dusting

4 tbsp sun-dried tomato paste

4 tomatoes, skinned and thinly sliced

2 red onions, chopped finely

4 slices prosciutto or other cooked ham, coarsely shredded

12 slices pepperoni sausage

12 black olives

3/4 tsp dried oregano

2 oz/55 g mozzarella cheese, grated

salt

pepperoni & onion pizza

Preheat the oven to 425°F/220°C. Brush a cookie sheet with oil.

Roll out the dough on a lightly floured counter to a 10-inch/ 25-cm round. Place on the cookie sheet and push up the edge a little. Cover and let stand in a warm place for 10 minutes.

Spread the sun-dried tomato paste evenly over the base. Arrange the tomato slices on the base and season with salt. Sprinkle over the chopped onion and prosciutto and arrange the pepperoni on top. Add the olives and sprinkle with oregano. Then add the grated cheese, and drizzle with olive oil.

Bake in the oven for 20–30 minutes, until golden and sizzling. Serve immediately.

serves 2–4

2 tbsp olive oil, plus extra for brushing

1 quantity Pizza Dough (see page 11), or 1 x 10-inch/ 25-cm pizza base

all-purpose flour, for dusting

2 shallots, thinly sliced

1 yellow bell pepper, seeded and cut into thin strips

4 oz/115 g cremini mushrooms, thinly sliced

12 oz/350 g skinless, boneless chicken breast portions, cut into thin strips

2 tbsp olive oil

2 tbsp chopped fresh parsley

1¹/2 cups grated mozzarella cheese

salt and pepper

chicken & mushroom pizza

Preheat the oven to 400°F/200°C. Brush a cookie sheet with oil.

Roll out the dough on a lightly floured counter to a 10-inch/ 25-cm round. Place on the cookie sheet and push up the edge a little. Cover and let stand in a warm place for 10 minutes.

Heat the olive oil in a wok or large skillet. Add the shallots, bell pepper, mushrooms, and chicken and stir-fry over medium-high heat for 4–5 minutes. Season to taste. Remove the mixture with a slotted spoon and let cool.

Brush the pizza with half the olive oil. Stir the parsley into the chicken and mushroom mixture and spread it evenly over the pizza base almost to the edge. Sprinkle with the mozzarella, drizzle over the remaining olive oil, and bake for 20 minutes, until the edge is crisp and golden. Serve immediately.

serves 2–4

2 tbsp olive oil, plus extra for brushing

1 quantity Pizza Dough (see page 11), or 1 x 10-inch/ 25-cm pizza base

all-purpose flour, for dusting

7 oz/200 g chorizo or other spicy sausages

2/3 cup freshly grated Parmesan cheese

14 oz/400 g canned chopped tomatoes

4 oz/115 g pancetta or bacon, cut into thin slices

1 tbsp fresh basil leaves

sausage pizza

Preheat the oven to 400°F/200°C. Brush a cookie sheet with oil.

Roll out the dough on a lightly floured counter to a 10-inch/ 25-cm round. Place on the cookie sheet and push up the edge a little. Cover and let stand in a warm place for 10 minutes.

Remove and discard the sausage casings and crumble the meat into a bowl. Add the Parmesan and mix well.

Spoon the tomatoes evenly over the pizza base almost to the edge, then sprinkle with the sausage mixture. Top with the pancetta and basil leaves and drizzle with the olive oil. Bake for 20 minutes, until the edge is crisp and golden. Serve immediately.

serves 2–4

2 tbsp olive oil, plus extra for brushing

1 bunch of scallions, chopped

2 garlic cloves, finely chopped

8 oz/225 g ground beef

1 tsp chili powder

7 oz/200 g canned chopped tomatoes

1/2 tsp Tabasco sauce

7 oz/200 g canned red kidney beans, drained and rinsed

1 quantity Pizza Dough (see page 11), or 1 x 10-inch/ 25-cm pizza base

all-purpose flour, for dusting

2–3 jalapeño chiles, thinly sliced

1 1/4 cups grated mozzarella cheese

salt and pepper

chili pizza

Heat the oil in a pan. Add the scallions and cook over medium-low heat, stirring occasionally, for 4–5 minutes, until softened. Add the garlic, ground beef, and chili powder and cook, stirring occasionally, for 5 minutes, until browned. Stir in the tomatoes and Tabasco and bring to a boil. Lower the heat, cover, and simmer for 30 minutes, then remove the pan from the heat, stir in the beans, season with salt and pepper, and let cool.

Preheat the oven to 400°F/200°C. Brush a cookie sheet with oil.

Roll out the dough on a lightly floured counter to a 10-inch/ 25-cm round. Place on the cookie sheet and push up the edge a little. Cover and let stand in a warm place for 10 minutes.

Spoon the meat mixture evenly over the pizza base almost to the edge. Sprinkle with the chiles and mozzarella and bake for 20 minutes, until the edge is crisp and golden. Serve immediately.

serves 2–4

2 tbsp olive oil, plus extra for
brushing

1 quantity Pizza Dough
(see page 11), or 1 x 10-inch/
25-cm pizza base

all-purpose flour, for dusting

2 tbsp sun-dried tomato
paste

5 oz/150 g mozzarella cheese,
torn into small pieces

14 oz/400 g canned chopped
tomatoes

2$^{1}/_{2}$ oz/70 g ham, cut into
thin strips

2 garlic cloves, finely
chopped

$^{1}/_{2}$ red bell pepper, seeded
and thinly sliced

6 pitted black olives, halved

1 tbsp fresh basil leaves

2 tbsp freshly grated
Parmesan cheese

ham & tomato pizza

Preheat the oven to 400°F/200°C. Brush a cookie sheet with oil.

Roll out the dough on a lightly floured counter to a 10-inch/
25-cm round. Place on the cookie sheet and push up the edge a
little. Cover and let stand in a warm place for 10 minutes.

Spread the sun-dried tomato paste over the base almost to the
edge. Sprinkle with half the mozzarella. Spoon the tomatoes
evenly over the top, then sprinkle with the ham, garlic, bell
pepper, olives, and basil leaves.

Add the remaining mozzarella, drizzle with the olive oil, and
sprinkle evenly with the Parmesan. Bake for 20 minutes, until
the edge is crisp and golden. Serve immediately.

serves 2–4

2 tbsp olive oil, plus extra for brushing

1 quantity Pizza Dough (see page 11), or 1 x 10-inch/ 25-cm pizza base

all-purpose flour, for dusting

5 tbsp basic Tomato Sauce (see page 7)

5 oz/150 g pepperoni, sliced

4–5 jalapeño chiles in brine, drained and thinly sliced

1 small green bell pepper, seeded and cut into thin strips

2 oz/55 g mozzarella cheese, sliced

1/2 cup grated Monterey jack cheese

extra-spicy pepperoni pizza

Preheat the oven to 400°F/200°C. Brush a cookie sheet with oil.

Roll out the dough on a lightly floured counter to a 10-inch/ 25-cm round. Place on the cookie sheet and push up the edge a little. Cover and let stand in a warm place for 10 minutes.

Spread the Tomato Sauce evenly over the base almost to the edge. Arrange the pepperoni slices on top and sprinkle with the chiles and bell pepper. Arrange the mozzarella slices over the pepperoni and sprinkle with the Monterey jack.

Drizzle with the olive oil and bake for 20 minutes, until the edge is crisp and golden. Serve immediately.

serves 2–4

9 oz/250 g flaky pastry dough, well chilled

all-purpose flour, for dusting

3 tbsp butter

1 red onion, chopped

1 garlic clove, chopped

1/3 cup white bread flour

1 1/4 cups milk

scant 2/3 cup finely grated Parmesan cheese, plus extra for sprinkling

2 eggs, hard-cooked, cut into fourths

3 1/2 oz/100 g Italian pork sausage, such as feline salame, cut into strips

salt and pepper

fresh thyme sprigs, to garnish

mini creamy ham pizzas

Fold the pastry dough in half and evenly grate it into 4 individual tart pans measuring 4 inches/10 cm wide. Using a floured fork, gently press the dough flakes down, making sure that there are no holes, and that the dough comes up the sides of the pans.

Line with foil and bake blind in a preheated oven, 425°F/220°C, for 10 minutes. Reduce the heat to 400°F/200°C, remove the foil from the pizza shells, and cook for 15 minutes, or until golden and set.

Heat the butter in a skillet. Add the onion and garlic and cook for 5–6 minutes, or until softened.

Add the flour, stirring well to coat the onion. Gradually stir in the milk to make a thick sauce.

Season the sauce with salt and pepper to taste and then stir in the Parmesan cheese. Do not reheat once the cheese has been added or the sauce will become too stringy.

Spread the sauce evenly over the cooked pizza shells. Decorate with the eggs and strips of sausage.

Sprinkle with a little extra Parmesan cheese, return to the oven, and bake for 5 minutes just to heat through.

Serve immediately, garnished with sprigs of fresh thyme.

serves 2–4

2 tbsp olive oil, plus extra for brushing

2–4 fresh or pickled jalapeño chiles, thinly sliced

1 quantity Pizza Dough (see page 11), or 1 x 10-inch/ 25-cm pizza base

all-purpose flour, for dusting

1/2–3/4 cup smoky barbecue sauce

4 tomatoes, sliced

1/2 cup diced smoked ham

3/4 cup thinly sliced pepperoni

1/2 cup grated Gruyère cheese

salt

chicago pepperoni pizza

Preheat the oven to 400°F/200°C. Brush a cookie sheet with oil. Seed the chiles if you prefer a milder flavor.

Roll out the dough on a lightly floured counter to a 10-inch/ 25-cm round. Place on the cookie sheet and push up the edge a little. Cover and let stand in a warm place for 10 minutes.

Brush the pizza base with half the oil, then spread the barbecue sauce evenly over it almost to the edge. Arrange the tomato slices over the base and season with salt, then sprinkle with the smoked ham. Cover with the pepperoni slices, top with the chiles, and sprinkle with the cheese. Drizzle with the remaining oil and bake for 20–25 minutes, until crisp and golden. Serve immediately.

serves 2–4

4 tbsp olive oil, plus extra for brushing

1/3 cup diced smoked bacon

1 onion, finely chopped

10 oz/280 g skinless boneless chicken breast portions, cut into strips

1 tsp chopped fresh tarragon

4 oz/115 g sliced smoked chicken, cut into strips

1 1/2 quantity Pizza Dough (see page 11), or 1 x 15-inch/ 38-cm pizza base

all-purpose flour for dusting

pinch of dried oregano

1 1/4 cups grated mozzarella cheese

deep dish chicken feast pizza

Heat 2 tbsp of the oil with the bacon in a skillet. Add the onion and cook over low heat, stirring occasionally, for 5 minutes, until softened. Add the fresh chicken strips, increase the heat to medium, and stir-fry for 4–5 minutes, until lightly browned on the outside.

Remove the skillet from the heat and drain off as much oil as possible. Stir in the tarragon and smoked chicken and let the mixture cool completely.

Preheat the oven to 425°F/220°C. Brush a cookie sheet or deep pizza pan with oil.

Roll out the dough on a lightly floured counter to a 15-inch/ 38-cm round. Place on the cookie sheet, push up the edge, and roll it over. Cover and let stand in a warm place for 10 minutes.

Brush the pizza base with 1 tablespoon of the remaining oil, then spoon in the chicken mixture and sprinkle with the oregano. Drizzle with the remaining oil and sprinkle with the mozzarella. Bake for 25–30 minutes, until golden. Serve immediately.

serves 2–4

5 tbsp olive oil, plus extra for brushing

2 onions, thinly sliced

3 tbsp butter

1 tbsp all-purpose flour, plus extra for dusting

1/2 cup milk

pinch of grated nutmeg

7 oz/200 g lean ground beef

3 tbsp finely chopped ham

1 tbsp chopped fresh flat-leaf parsley

1/3 cup grated Parmesan cheese

1 egg yolk

1 quantity Pizza Dough (see page 11), or 1 x 10-inch/ 25-cm pizza base

3/4 cup strained canned tomatoes or 1 quantity basic Tomato Sauce (see page 7)

8 black olives

1 cup grated mozzarella cheese

salt and pepper

meatball pizza

Heat 2 tbsp of the oil in a skillet. Add the onions and cook over low heat, stirring occasionally, for 15–20 minutes, until golden brown.

Meanwhile, make a béchamel sauce. Melt 1 tbsp of the butter in a small pan. Stir in the flour and cook, stirring constantly, for 1 minute. Gradually stir in the milk and bring to a boil, stirring constantly. Cook, stirring, for 1–2 minutes more, until thickened. Remove the pan from the heat and stir in a small pinch of nutmeg.

Combine the ground beef, ham, parsley, Parmesan, and egg yolk in a bowl and season. Add 1–2 tbsp of the béchamel and bring the mixture together. Shape into about 12 small balls and dust lightly with flour. Melt the remaining butter with 1 tbsp of the remaining oil in another skillet. Add the meatballs and cook over medium heat, turning frequently, for 4–5 minutes, until browned all over. Remove with a slotted spoon and set aside.

Preheat the oven to 400°F/200°C. Brush a cookie sheet with oil.

Roll out the dough on a lightly floured counter to a 10-inch/ 25-cm round. Place on the cookie sheet and push up the edge a little. Cover and let stand in a warm place for 10 minutes. Brush the pizza base with half the remaining olive oil. Spread the strained canned tomatoes or Tomato Sauce over the base almost to the edge. Using a slotted spoon, put the onions evenly over the top. Arrange the meatballs on the onions and add the olives, then sprinkle with the mozzarella, and drizzle with the remaining oil. Bake for 20 minutes, until crisp and golden. Serve immediately.

Strictly Vegetarian

serves 2–4

4 garlic cloves

2 red onions, cut into wedges

1 orange bell pepper, seeded and cut into 8 strips

1 yellow bell pepper, seeded and cut into 8 strips

4 baby zucchini, halved lengthwise

4 baby eggplants, cut lengthwise into 4 slices

1/2 cup olive oil, plus extra for brushing

1 tbsp balsamic vinegar

2 tbsp fresh basil leaves

1 quantity Pizza Dough (see page 11), or 1 x 10-inch/ 25-cm pizza base

all-purpose flour, for dusting

1 quantity basic Tomato Sauce (see page 7)

6 oz/175 g goat cheese, diced

salt and pepper

roasted vegetable pizza

Preheat the oven to 400°F/200°C. Brush a cookie sheet with oil.

Spread the garlic, onions, bell peppers, zucchini, and eggplants in a roasting pan. Season to taste with salt and pepper. Mix the oil, vinegar, and basil together in a pitcher and pour the mixture over the vegetables, tossing well to coat. Roast in the preheated oven for 15 minutes, turning once or twice during cooking. Let cool. Increase the oven temperature to 425°F/220°C.

Roll out the dough on a lightly floured counter to a 10-inch/ 25-cm round. Place on the cookie sheet and push up the edge a little. Cover and let stand in a warm place for 10 minutes. Add the Tomato Sauce, spreading it almost to the edges. Peel off the skins from the bell pepper strips. Peel and slice the garlic. Arrange the vegetables on top of the tomato sauce, then sprinkle with the goat cheese. Drizzle over the roasting juices.

Bake in the oven for 15–20 minutes, or until golden. Garnish with fresh basil and serve immediately.

serves 8

1 quantity Pizza Dough
(see page 11) or 1 x 10-inch/
25-cm pizza base

all-purpose flour, for dusting

2 tbsp olive oil, plus extra for
oiling and drizzling

1/2 red bell pepper seeded
and thinly sliced

1/2 green bell pepper, seeded
and thinly sliced

1/2 yellow bell pepper, seeded
and thinly sliced

1 small red onion, thinly
sliced

1 garlic clove, crushed

1 quantity basic Tomato
Sauce (see page 7)

3 tbsp golden raisins

4 tbsp pine nuts

1 tbsp chopped fresh thyme

salt and pepper

bell pepper & onion pizza fingers

Roll out or press the dough, using a rolling pin or your hands, on a lightly floured counter to fit a 12 x 7 inch/30 x 18 cm oiled jelly roll pan. Place the dough in the pan and push up the edges slightly.

Cover with plastic wrap and set the dough aside in a warm place for about 10 minutes to rise slightly.

Heat the oil in a large skillet. Add the bell peppers, onion, and garlic and cook gently for 5 minutes until they have softened. Set aside to cool.

Spread the Tomato Sauce over the base of the pizza almost to the edge.

Sprinkle over the golden raisins and top with the cooled bell pepper mixture. Add the pine nuts and thyme. Drizzle with a little olive oil and season to taste with salt and pepper.

Bake in a preheated oven, 400°F/200°C, for 18–20 minutes, or until the edges are crisp and golden. Cut into fingers and serve immediately.

serves 2–4

3 tbsp oil

1 quantity Pizza Dough
(see page 11), or 1 x 10-inch/
25-cm pizza base

all-purpose flour, for dusting

2 garlic cloves, crushed

2 tbsp chopped fresh oregano

3/4 cup curd cheese

1 tbsp milk

3 tbsp butter

12 oz/350 g mixed
mushrooms, sliced

2 tsp lemon juice

1 tbsp chopped fresh
marjoram

4 tbsp freshly grated
Parmesan cheese

salt and pepper

mixed mushroom pizza

Preheat the oven to 475°F/240°C. Brush a cookie sheet with oil.

Roll out the dough on a lightly floured counter to a 10-inch/
25-cm round. Place on the cookie sheet and push up the edge a
little. Cover and let stand in a warm place for 10 minutes.

Mix 2 tablespoons of the oil, the garlic, and oregano together and
brush over the pizza base.

Mix the curd cheese and milk together in a bowl. Season to taste
with salt and pepper and spread the mixture over the pizza base,
leaving a 1½-inch/4-cm border.

Heat the butter and remaining oil together in a large skillet. Add
the mushrooms and cook over high heat for 2 minutes. Remove
the skillet from the heat, season to taste with salt and pepper,
and stir in the lemon juice and marjoram.

Spoon the mushroom mixture over the pizza base, leaving a
½-inch/1-cm border. Sprinkle with the grated Parmesan cheese,
then bake in the oven for 12–15 minutes, until the crust is crisp
and the mushrooms are cooked. Serve immediately.

serves 2–4

olive oil, for brushing

1 quantity Pizza Dough
(see page 11), or 1 x 10-inch/
25-cm pizza base

all-purpose flour, for dusting

4 tbsp sun-dried tomato
paste

2/3 cup ricotta cheese

10 sun-dried tomatoes in oil,
drained

1 tbsp fresh thyme

salt and pepper

tomato & ricotta pizza

Preheat the oven to 400°F/200°C. Brush a cookie sheet with oil.

Roll out the dough on a lightly floured counter to a 10-inch/
25-cm round. Place on the cookie sheet and push up the edge a
little. Cover and let stand in a warm place for 10 minutes.

Spread the sun-dried tomato paste evenly over the dough, then
add spoonfuls of ricotta cheese, dotting them over the pizza.

Cut the drained sun-dried tomatoes into strips and arrange
these on top of the pizza.

Sprinkle the thyme over the top of the pizza and season with
salt and pepper to taste. Bake in a preheated oven, 400°F/200°C,
for 30 minutes or until piping hot and the crust is golden. Serve
the pizza at once.

serves 4

4 ready-made, pre-cooked individual pizza bases

1 tbsp olive oil

7 oz/200 g canned chopped tomatoes with garlic and herbs

2 tbsp tomato paste

7 oz/200 g canned kidney beans, drained and rinsed

2/3 cup corn kernels, thawed if frozen

1–2 tsp chili sauce

1 large red onion, shredded

1 cup grated sharp colby cheese

1 large fresh green chile, seeded and sliced into rings

salt and pepper

mexican pizzas

Arrange the ready-made pizza bases on a large cookie sheet and brush the surfaces lightly with the olive oil.

Combine the chopped tomatoes, tomato paste, kidney beans, and corn in a large bowl and add chili sauce to taste. Season to taste with salt and pepper.

Spread the tomato and kidney bean mixture evenly over each of the pizza bases.

Top each pizza with shredded onion and sprinkle with some grated cheese and a few slices of fresh green chile to taste.

Bake in a preheated oven, 425°F/220°C, for 20 minutes, until the vegetables are tender, the cheese has melted, and the pizza dough is crisp and golden.

Remove the pizzas from the cookie sheet and transfer to serving plates. Serve hot.

serves 2–4

6 spinach leaves

olive oil, for brushing and drizzling

1 quantity Pizza Dough (see page 11), or 1 x 10-inch/ 25-cm pizza base

all-purpose flour, for dusting

1 quantity basic Tomato Sauce (see page 7)

1 tomato, sliced

1 celery stalk, thinly sliced

1/2 green bell pepper, seeded and thinly sliced

1 baby zucchini, sliced

1 oz/25 g asparagus tips

2 1/2 tbsp corn, thawed if frozen

4 tbsp peas, thawed if frozen

4 scallions, trimmed and chopped

1 tbsp chopped fresh mixed herbs

1/2 cup grated mozzarella cheese

2 tbsp freshly grated Parmesan cheese

1 artichoke heart

salt and pepper

vegetable pizza

Remove any tough stalks from the spinach and wash the leaves in cold water. Pat dry with paper towels.

Preheat the oven to 400°F/200°C. Brush a cookie sheet with oil.

Roll out the dough on a lightly floured counter to a 10-inch/ 25-cm round. Place on the cookie sheet and push up the edge a little. Cover and let stand in a warm place for 10 minutes.

Spread the Tomato Sauce over the base of the pizza almost to the edge. Arrange the spinach leaves on the sauce, followed by the tomato slices. Top with the remaining vegetables and the fresh mixed herbs.

Combine the cheeses and sprinkle over the pizza. Place the artichoke heart in the center. Drizzle the pizza with a little olive oil and season to taste.

Bake in the oven for 18–20 minutes or until the edge is crisp and golden brown. Serve immediately.

serves 2–4

1/4 cup drained sun-dried tomatoes in oil, coarsely chopped

4 tbsp pine nuts

1/2 cup fresh basil leaves

1 garlic clove, chopped

5 tbsp olive oil, plus extra for brushing

2 tbsp grated Parmesan cheese

1 quantity Pizza Dough (see page 11), or 1 x 10-inch/ 25-cm pizza base

all-purpose flour, for dusting

3 oz/85 g goat cheese

3 oz/85 g red cherry tomatoes, halved

3 oz/85 g yellow cherry tomatoes, halved

salt and pepper

basil, to garnish

goat cheese & sun-dried tomato pizza

Put the sun-dried tomatoes, pine nuts, basil, and garlic in a food processor or blender and process to a purée. With the motor running, gradually add the olive oil through the feeder tube or hole until thoroughly combined. Scrape into a bowl and stir in the Parmesan. Alternatively, pound the sun-dried tomatoes, pine nuts, basil, and garlic to a paste in a mortar with a pestle. Gradually beat in the oil, then stir in the Parmesan. Season lightly with salt and pepper.

Preheat the oven to 400°F/200°C. Brush a cookie sheet with oil.

Roll out the dough on a lightly floured counter to a 10-inch/ 25-cm round. Place on the cookie sheet and push up the edge a little. Cover and let stand in a warm place for 10 minutes.

Spread the sun-dried tomato mixture over the pizza base almost to the edge. Crumble the goat cheese over it and arrange the tomato halves on top. Bake for 20 minutes, until crisp and golden. Garnish with basil and serve immediately.

serves 2–4

2 tbsp olive oil, plus extra for brushing and drizzling

1 quantity Pizza Dough (see page 11), or 1 x 10-inch/ 25-cm pizza base

all-purpose flour, for dusting

12 oz/350 g spinach

1 onion, thinly sliced

6 tbsp ricotta cheese

1/2 tsp freshly grated nutmeg

2 tbsp pine nuts

4 oz/115 g Fontina cheese, thinly sliced

salt and pepper

ricotta, spinach, & pine nut pizza

Preheat the oven to 425°F/220°C. Brush a cookie sheet with oil.

Roll out the dough on a lightly floured counter to a 10-inch/ 25-cm round. Place on the cookie sheet and push up the edge a little. Cover and let stand in a warm place for 10 minutes.

Wash the spinach in cold water and dry well. Heat the oil in a skillet, add the onion and cook until soft and translucent. Add the spinach and cook, stirring, until just wilted. Remove the skillet from the heat and drain off any liquid.

Spread the ricotta cheese evenly over the pizza base, then cover with the spinach and onion mixture. Sprinkle over the nutmeg and pine nuts and season to taste with salt and pepper. Top with the slices of Fontina and drizzle with olive oil. Bake in the oven for 20–30 minutes, until golden and sizzling. Serve immediately.

serves 2–4

2 tbsp olive oil, plus extra for brushing and drizzling

1 quantity Pizza Dough (see page 11), or 1 x 10-inch/ 25-cm pizza base

all-purpose flour, for dusting

1 quantity basic Tomato Sauce (see page 7)

1/2 cup soft cheese

1 tbsp chopped fresh mixed herbs, such as parsley, oregano, and basil

8 oz/225 g exotic mushrooms, such as oyster, shiitake, or ceps, or 4 oz/115 g each exotic and white mushrooms

1/4 tsp fennel seeds

4 tbsp coarsely chopped walnuts

1 1/2 oz/40 g blue cheese

salt and pepper

mushroom & walnut pizza

Preheat the oven to 400°F/200°C. Brush a cookie sheet with oil.

Roll out the dough on a lightly floured counter to a 10-inch/ 25-cm round. Place on the cookie sheet and push up the edge a little. Cover and let stand in a warm place for 10 minutes.

Carefully spread the Tomato Sauce almost to the edge of the pizza base. Dot with the soft cheese and chopped fresh herbs.

Wipe and slice the mushrooms. Heat the oil in a large skillet or wok and stir-fry the mushrooms and fennel seeds for 2–3 minutes. Spread over the pizza with the walnuts.

Crumble the blue cheese over the pizza, drizzle with a little olive oil, and season with salt and pepper to taste.

Bake in the oven for 18–20 minutes or until the edge is crisp and golden. Serve immediately

serves 2–4

olive oil, for brushing

1 quantity Pizza Dough
(see page 11), or 1 x 10-inch/
25-cm pizza base

all-purpose flour, for dusting

7 oz/200 g canned chopped
tomatoes

sliced tomatoes

1 garlic clove, finely chopped

1 bay leaf

1/2 tsp dried oregano

1/2 tsp sugar

1 tsp balsamic vinegar

salt and pepper

1 eggplant, thinly sliced

2 tbsp olive oil

6 oz/175 g mozzarella cheese,
sliced

2 oz/55 g marinated, pitted
black olives

1 tbsp drained capers

4 tbsp freshly grated
Parmesan cheese

pizza alla siciliana

Preheat the oven to 400°F/200°C. To make the tomato sauce, place all the ingredients in a heavy-bottomed pan, season to taste, and bring to a boil. Reduce the heat and simmer, stirring occasionally, for about 20 minutes, or until thickened and reduced. Remove from the heat, discard the bay leaf, and let cool.

Brush a cookie sheet with oil.

Roll out the dough on a lightly floured counter to a 10-inch/ 25-cm round. Place on the cookie sheet and push up the edge a little. Cover and let stand in a warm place for 10 minutes.

Spread the tomato sauce over the pizza base almost to the edge. Arrange the eggplant on top and cover with mozzarella. Top with olives and capers and sprinkle with Parmesan. Drizzle with the olive oil. Bake for 15–20 minutes, or until golden. Serve immediately.

Something Special

makes 4

2 tbsp olive oil, plus extra for
brushing

1 red onion, thinly sliced

1 garlic clove, finely chopped

14 oz/400 g canned tomatoes,
chopped

1/3 cup black olives, pitted

2 quantities Pizza Dough
(see page 11)

all-purpose flour, for dusting

7 oz/200 g mozzarella cheese,
drained and diced

1 tbsp chopped fresh oregano

salt and pepper

pizza calzone

To make the filling, heat the olive oil in a skillet. Add the
onion and garlic and cook over low heat, stirring occasionally,
for 5 minutes, until softened. Add the tomatoes and cook,
stirring occasionally, for an additional 5 minutes. Stir in the
olives and season to taste with salt and pepper. Remove the
skillet from the heat.

Divide the dough into 4 pieces. Roll out each piece on a lightly
floured counter to form an 8-inch/20-cm circle.

Divide the tomato mixture between the circles, spreading it over
half of each almost to the edge. Top with the cheese and sprinkle
with the oregano. Brush the edge of each circle with a little
water and fold over the uncovered sides. Press the edges to seal.

Transfer the turnovers to lightly oiled baking sheets and bake
in a preheated oven, 400°F/200°C, for about 15 minutes, until
golden and crisp. Remove from the oven and let stand for
2 minutes, then transfer to warmed plates and serve.

serves 2–4

2 tbsp olive oil, plus extra for brushing and drizzling

1 small onion, finely chopped

1 garlic clove, finely chopped

1 green bell pepper, seeded and chopped

8 oz/225 g plum tomatoes, peeled and chopped

1 tbsp tomato paste

1 tsp soft brown sugar

1 tbsp shredded fresh basil leaves

1 bay leaf

1 quantity Pizza Dough (see page 11), or 1 x 10-inch/25-cm pizza base

all-purpose flour, for dusting

2¹/₂ oz/70 g cooked shelled shrimp

2 oz/55 g artichoke hearts, thinly sliced

1 oz/25 g mozzarella cheese, drained and thinly sliced

1 tomato, thinly sliced

3¹/₂ oz/100 g mushrooms or pepperoni, thinly sliced

2 tsp capers, rinsed

2 tsp pitted, sliced black olives

2 tbsp olive oil, plus extra for brushing

salt and pepper

four seasons pizza

To make the tomato sauce, heat the olive oil in a heavy-bottom pan. Add the onion, garlic, and bell pepper, and cook over low heat, stirring occasionally, for 5 minutes, until softened. Add the tomatoes, tomato paste, sugar, basil, and bay leaf, and season to taste with salt and pepper. Cover and let simmer, stirring occasionally, for 30 minutes, until thickened. Remove the pan from the heat and let the sauce cool completely.

Roll out the dough on a lightly floured counter to a 10-inch/25-cm round. Place on the cookie sheet and push up the edge a little. Cover and let stand in a warm place for 10 minutes.

Spread the tomato sauce over the pizza base, almost to the edge. Cover one quarter of each with shrimp. Cover a second quarter with artichoke hearts. Cover the third quarter with alternate slices of mozzarella and tomato. Cover the final quarter with sliced mushrooms or pepperoni. Sprinkle the surface with capers and olives, season to taste with salt and pepper, and drizzle with the olive oil.

Bake in a preheated oven, 425°F/220°C, for 20–25 minutes, until the crust is crisp and the cheese has melted. Serve immediately.

makes two 9 inch/23 cm pizzas

1 cup/225 ml water

3 1/2 cups all-purpose flour, plus extra for dusting

1 envelope active dry yeast

1 tsp salt

1 tbsp extra-virgin olive oil, plus extra for brushing

2 zucchini

10 1/2 oz/300 g buffalo mozzarella

1 1/2–2 tbsp finely chopped fresh rosemary, or 1/2 tbsp dried rosemary

pizza biancas

To make the crust, heat the water in the microwave on high for 1 minute or until it reads 125°F/52°C on an instant-read thermometer. Alternatively, heat the water in a pan over low heat until it is lukewarm.

Stir the flour, yeast, and salt together and make a well in the center. Stir in most of the water with the olive oil to make a dough. Add the remaining water, if necessary, to form a soft dough. Turn out onto a lightly floured counter and knead for about 10 minutes until smooth but still soft. Wash and dry the bowl and lightly coat with olive oil. Shape the dough into a ball, put in the bowl, and turn the dough over so it is coated. Cover and set aside until doubled in size.

Turn the dough out onto a lightly floured counter. Quickly knead a few times, then cover with the upturned bowl, and set aside for 10 minutes.

Meanwhile, using a vegetable peeler, cut long, thin strips of zucchini. Drain and dice the mozzarella.

Divide the dough in half and shape each half into a ball. Cover 1 ball and roll out the other into a 9-inch/23-cm round. Place the round on a lightly floured cookie sheet.

Scatter half the mozzarella over the base. Add half the zucchini strips and sprinkle with half the rosemary. Repeat with the remaining dough and remaining topping ingredients.

Bake in a preheated oven, 425°F/ 220°C, for 15 minutes or until crispy. Serve immediately.

serves 2–4

olive oil, for brushing

1 quantity Pizza Dough (see page 11), or 1 x 10-inch/ 25-cm pizza base

all-purpose flour, for dusting

1/2 cup chopped fresh parsley

1/2 cup chopped fresh basil

1/4 cup chopped fresh chives

1/4 cup chopped fresh marjoram

2 garlic cloves, finely chopped

1/2 cup sour cream

1 tbsp olive oil flavored with mixed herbs

11/3 cups freshly grated Parmesan cheese

salt and pepper

mixed herbs pizza

Preheat the oven to 400°F/200°C. Brush a cookie sheet with oil.

Roll out the dough on a lightly floured counter to a 10-inch/ 25-cm round. Place on the cookie sheet and push up the edge a little. Cover and let stand in a warm place for 10 minutes.

Combine the parsley, basil, chives, marjoram, garlic, and sour cream in a bowl and season with salt and pepper. Brush the pizza base with the flavored oil, then spread the herb mixture evenly over it almost to the edge. Sprinkle with the Parmesan and bake for 20 minutes, until crisp and golden. Serve immediately.

serves 2–4

6 tbsp olive oil, plus extra for brushing

10¹/2 oz/300 g onions, halved and thinly sliced

1/4 cup dry white wine

1 tbsp white wine vinegar

1 tsp lemon juice

1¹/4 cups chopped arugula

2 tbsp pine nuts

2 garlic cloves, chopped

2/3 cup freshly grated Parmesan cheese

1 quantity Pizza Dough (see page 11), or 1 x 10-inch/ 25-cm pizza base

all-purpose flour, for dusting

8 oz/225 g mozzarella cheese, diced

2 tbsp chopped fresh parsley

salt and pepper

caramelized onion & arugula pesto pizza

Heat 2 tbsp of the oil in a heavy-based pan. Add the onions, cover, and cook over very low heat, stirring occasionally, for 1 hour. Increase the heat to medium, uncover the pan, and cook until all the liquid has evaporated and the onions are golden brown. Stir in the wine, vinegar, and lemon juice, season with salt and pepper, and cook, stirring constantly, until the liquid has almost evaporated. Remove the pan from the heat.

Meanwhile, put the arugula, pine nuts, and garlic in a food processor or blender and process to a purée. With the motor running, gradually add 3 tablespoons of the remaining olive oil through the feeder tube or hole until thoroughly combined. Scrape into a bowl and stir in the Parmesan. Alternatively, pound the arugula, pine nuts, and garlic to a paste in a mortar with a pestle. Gradually beat in the oil, then stir in the Parmesan. Season with salt and pepper.

Preheat the oven to 400°F/200°C. Brush a cookie sheet with oil. Roll out the dough on a lightly floured counter to a 10-inch/ 25-cm round. Place on the cookie sheet and push up the edge a little. Cover and let stand in a warm place for 10 minutes.

Spread the caramelized onions evenly over the pizza base almost to the edge. Sprinkle with the mozzarella and then with the parsley. Drizzle with the remaining olive oil and bake for 20 minutes, until crisp and golden. Serve immediately.

makes 10

1 quantity Pizza Dough (see page 11)

all-purpose flour, for dusting

3/4 cup strained canned tomatoes or 1 quantity basic Tomato Sauce (see page 7)

3 oz/85 g mozzarella cheese, diced

3 oz/85 g sliced ham, salami, or smoked chicken, cut into strips

2 fresh marjoram sprigs, chopped

4 cups peanut oil

deep-fried pizza sandwiches

Divide the dough into 10 pieces and roll out each piece to a round on a lightly floured counter.

Spread the strained canned tomatoes or Tomato Sauce evenly over the rounds, leaving a ¾-inch margin around the edges. Divide the cheese, meat, and marjoram among the rounds. Brush the margins of the rounds with water, fold over the dough, and press the edges firmly to seal.

Heat the oil in a deep-fryer or heavy pan to 350–375°F/180–190°C or until a cube of day-old bread browns in 30 seconds. Add the pizza sandwiches, in batches, and cook for 10 minutes, until crisp and golden brown. Drain well on paper towels and keep warm while cooking the remaining batches. Serve hot.

serves 2–4

3 tablespoons olive oil

1 onion, chopped

2 garlic cloves, chopped

1 sliced cups mushrooms

1 quantity Pizza Dough
(see page 11)

all-purpose flour, for dusting

generous 1 cup drained
canned corn

7 oz/200 g canned chopped
tomatoes

4 oz/115 g pepperoni sausage,
sliced

1/2 cup grated Cheddar
cheese

pinch of dried oregano

salt and pepper

upside-down pizza

Heat 2 tbsp of the oil in a 10-inch skillet. Add the onion and cook over low heat, stirring occasionally, for 5 minutes. Add the garlic and mushrooms and cook, stirring occasionally, for 5 minutes more. Remove the skillet from the heat, drain off the oil, and let cool.

Preheat the oven to 400°F/200°C.

Roll out the dough on a lightly floured counter to a 10-inch round. Cover and let stand in a warm place for 10 minutes.

Stir the corn, tomatoes, pepperoni, cheese, and oregano into the onion mixture and season with salt and pepper. Place the dough round on top of the filling and tuck in the edge all the way around. Prick a few small holes in the dough to allow steam to escape during cooking and brush with the remaining olive oil. Bake for 18–20 minutes. (If the handle of your skillet cannot withstand the heat of the oven, transfer the mixture to a 10-inch baking pan before adding the dough.)

To serve, place a plate on top of the pizza and, holding the pan and plate firmly together, invert the two. Lift off the pan and serve the pizza immediately.

serves 2–4

olive oil, for brushing

1 quantity Pizza Dough
(see page 11), or 1 x 10-inch/
25-cm pizza base

all-purpose flour, for dusting

2 plum tomatoes, diced

2 shallots, diced

6 oz/175 g salmon fillet,
skinned and diced

salt and pepper

scant 1 cup strained plain
yogurt

4 scallions, finely chopped

1 mini cucumber, diced

1 garlic clove, finely chopped

2 tbsp chopped fresh mint

salmon & tzatziki pizza

Preheat the oven to 400°F/200°C. Brush a cookie sheet with oil.

Roll out the dough on a lightly floured counter to a 10-inch/
25-cm round. Place on the cookie sheet and push up the edge a
little. Cover and let stand in a warm place for 10 minutes.

Sprinkle the tomatoes and shallots evenly over the pizza base
almost to the edge. Top with the salmon and season with salt
and pepper. Bake for 20 minutes, until crisp and golden.

Meanwhile, make the tzatziki. Lightly whisk the yogurt with a
fork in a bowl. Stir in the scallions, cucumber, garlic, and mint
and season with salt and pepper.

Remove the pizza from the oven and top with a little of the
tzatziki. Serve immediately with the remaining tzatziki.

serves 2–4

1 fresh red chile

scant 1 cup canned coconut milk

1 tbsp red curry paste

1 tbsp soft dark brown sugar

1 tbsp Thai fish sauce

1 lemongrass stalk, lightly crushed

6 oz/175 g skinless boneless chicken breast portion, cut into strips

1/4 cup roasted peanuts, ground

oil, for brushing

1 quantity Pizza Dough (see page 11), or 1 x 10-inch/25-cm pizza base

all-purpose flour, for dusting

salt and pepper

fresh basil leaves, to garnish

thai curry pizza

Seed the chile if you prefer a milder flavor and slice thinly. Heat half the coconut milk in a heavy pan. Stir in the curry paste and cook, stirring, until it gives off its aroma. Add the sugar, fish sauce, and lemongrass and cook, stirring constantly, until the mixture is a rich golden brown color.

Add the remaining coconut milk and bring back to a boil, then stir in the chicken, peanuts, and chile. Lower the heat and simmer for 10–15 minutes, until most of the liquid has evaporated.

Meanwhile, preheat the oven to 400°F/200°C. Brush a cookie sheet with oil.

Roll out the dough on a lightly floured counter to a 10-inch/25-cm round. Place on the cookie sheet and push up the edge a little. Cover and let stand in a warm place for 10 minutes.

Remove the pan from the heat. Remove and discard the lemongrass and season the curry to taste with salt and pepper. Spoon the curry onto the pizza base, spreading it out almost to the edge. Bake for 20 minutes, until crisp and golden, and serve immediately, garnished with basil leaves.

serves 2–4

2 tbsp butter, plus extra for greasing

1 cup self-rising flour, plus extra for dusting

1/2 cup unsweetened cocoa powder

1/2 cup milk

3/4 cup farmer's cheese

scant 1/2 cup superfine sugar

1 medium egg, lightly beaten

1 tsp ground ginger

4 tbsp slivered almonds

7 oz/200 g canned or bottled Morello cherries, drained

chocolate pizza

Preheat the oven to 375°F/190°C. Grease a 10-inch shallow cake pan with butter.

To make the topping, combine the cheese, sugar, and egg in a bowl, beating well with a fork. Stir in the ground ginger and set aside.

To make the dough, sift together the flour and cocoa into another bowl. Add the butter and rub it in with your fingertips until the mixture resembles breadcrumbs. Make a well in the center and pour in 1/3 cup of the milk. Mix well with a round-bladed knife, adding the remaining milk if necessary to mix to a soft dough.

Turn out the dough onto a lightly floured counter and knead lightly. Roll out lightly to a 10¾-inch/27-cm round and lift into the pan, pressing it against the sides and evenly over the base.

Sprinkle half the almonds over the pizza base, add the cheese mixture, and bake for 15 minutes. Put the cherries on top of the cheese mixture, sprinkle with the remaining almonds, and return to the oven for 10–15 minutes more. Serve hot or cold.

almonds
    chocolate pizza 95
    Florentine pizza 26
anchovy pizza 25
artichoke hearts
    four seasons pizza 79
    vegetable pizza 65
arugula: caramelized onion & arugula pesto pizza 84
asparagus: vegetable pizza 65

bacon
    deep dish chicken feast pizza 48
    sausage pizza 36
    tasty bacon pizza 21
beef
    chili pizza 39
    meatball pizza 51
bell peppers
    bell pepper & onion pizza fingers 57
    chicken & mushroom pizza 35
    extra-spicy pepperoni pizza 43
    four seasons pizza 79
    ham & tomato pizza 40
    roasted vegetable pizza 54
    vegetable pizza 65

capers
    four seasons pizza 79
    pizza alla siciliana 73
    quattro formaggio pizza 22
cheese
    Chicago pepperoni pizza 47
    chocolate pizza 95
    extra-spicy pepperoni pizza 43
    Florentine pizza 26
    Hawaiian pizza 14
    Mexican pizzas 62
    mixed mushroom pizza 58
    mushroom & walnut pizza 70
    quattro formaggio pizza 22
    tasty bacon pizza 21
    upside-down pizza 88
    see also fontina cheese; goat cheese; mozzarella
        cheese; Parmesan cheese; ricotta cheese
cherries: chocolate pizza 95
chicken
    chicken & mushroom pizza 35
    deep-fried pizza sandwiches 87
    deep dish chicken feast pizza 48
    Thai curry pizza 92
chiles
    Chicago pepperoni pizza 47
    chili pizza 39
    extra-spicy pepperoni pizza 43
    Mexican pizzas 62
    Thai curry pizza 92
chocolate pizza 95
chorizo: sausage pizza 36
coconut milk: Thai curry pizza 92
corn
    Mexican pizzas 62
    upside-down pizza 88
    vegetable pizza 65

deep-fried pizza sandwiches 87

eggplants
    pizza alla siciliana 73
    roasted vegetable pizza 54
eggs
    Florentine pizza 26
    mini creamy ham pizzas 44

fontina cheese
    quattro formaggio pizza 22
    ricotta, spinach, & pine nut pizza 69
four seasons pizza 79

garlic mushroom pizza 17

goat cheese
    goat cheese & sun-dried tomato pizza 66
    quattro formaggio pizza 22
    roasted vegetable pizza 54

ham
    Chicago pepperoni pizza 47
    deep-fried pizza sandwiches 87
    ham & tomato pizza 40
    Hawaiian pizza 14
    meatball pizza 51
    pepperoni & onion pizza 32
Hawaiian pizza 14

kidney beans
    chili pizza 39
    Mexican pizzas 62

margarita pizza 13
Mexican pizzas 62
mixed herbs pizza 83
mozzarella cheese
    anchovy pizza 25
    caramelized onion & arugula pesto pizza 84
    chicken & mushroom pizza 35
    chili pizza 39
    deep-fried pizza sandwiches 87
    deep dish chicken feast pizza 48
    extra-spicy pepperoni pizza 43
    four seasons pizza 79
    garlic mushroom pizza 17
    ham & tomato pizza 40
    margarita pizza 13
    meatball pizza 51
    pepperoni & onion pizza 32
    pizza alla siciliana 73
    pizza biancas 80
    pizza calzone 76
    seafood pizza 29
    tomato & olive pizzas 18
    vegetable pizza 65
mushrooms
    chicken & mushroom pizza 35
    four seasons pizza 79
    garlic mushroom pizza 17
    mixed mushroom pizza 58
    mushroom & walnut pizza 70
    tasty bacon pizza 21
    upside-down pizza 88

olives
    anchovy pizza 25
    four seasons pizza 79
    ham & tomato pizza 40
    meatball pizza 51
    pepperoni & onion pizza 32
    pizza alla siciliana 73
    pizza calzone 76
    tomato & olive pizzas 18

Parmesan cheese
    caramelized onion & arugula pesto pizza 84
    Florentine pizza 26
    goat cheese & sun-dried tomato pizza 66
    ham & tomato pizza 40
    meatball pizza 51
    mini creamy ham pizzas 44
    mixed herbs pizza 83
    mixed mushroom pizza 58
    pizza alla siciliana 73
    quattro formaggio pizza 22
    sausage pizza 36
    vegetable pizza 65
peanuts: Thai curry pizza 92
pepperoni
    Chicago pepperoni pizza 47
    extra-spicy pepperoni pizza 43
    four seasons pizza 79

pepperoni & onion pizza 32
    upside-down pizza 88
pineapple: Hawaiian pizza 14
pine nuts
    bell pepper & onion pizza fingers 57
    caramelized onion & arugula pesto pizza 84
    goat cheese & sun-dried tomato pizza 66
    quattro formaggio pizza 22
    ricotta, spinach, & pine nut pizza 69
pizza dough 11

quattro formaggio pizza 22

red onions
    bell pepper & onion pizza fingers 57
    Florentine pizza 26
    Mexican pizzas 62
    pepperoni & onion pizza 32
    pizza calzone 76
    quattro formaggio pizza 22
    roasted vegetable pizza 54
ricotta cheese
    ricotta, spinach, & pine nut pizza 69
    tomato & ricotta pizza 61

salmon & tzatziki pizza 91
sausage
    mini creamy ham pizzas 44
    sausage pizza 36
    see also chorizo; pepperoni
seafood pizza 29
shrimp
    four seasons pizza 79
    seafood pizza 29
spinach
    Florentine pizza 26
    ricotta, spinach, & pine nut pizza 69
    vegetable pizza 65

Thai curry pizza 92
tomatoes
    anchovy pizza 25
    basic tomato sauce 7
    bell pepper & onion pizza fingers 57
    Chicago pepperoni pizza 47
    chili pizza 39
    deep-fried pizza sandwiches 87
    extra-spicy pepperoni pizza 43
    Florentine pizza 26
    four seasons pizza 79
    garlic mushroom pizza 17
    goat cheese & sun-dried tomato pizza 66
    ham & tomato pizza 40
    Hawaiian pizza 14
    margarita pizza 13
    meatball pizza 51
    Mexican pizzas 62
    mushroom & walnut pizza 70
    pepperoni & onion pizza 32
    pizza alla siciliana 73
    pizza calzone 76
    quattro formaggio pizza 22
    roasted vegetable pizza 54
    salmon & tzatziki pizza 91
    sausage pizza 36
    seafood pizza 29
    tomato & olive pizzas 18
    tomato & ricotta pizza 61
    upside-down pizza 88
    vegetable pizza 65
tuna: seafood pizza 29

walnuts: mushroom & walnut pizza 70

zucchini
    pizza biancas 80
    roasted vegetable pizza 54
    vegetable pizza 65